Copyright © 2019 Disney Enterprises, Inc. All rights reserved.

Published by Scholastic Australia in 2019.
Scholastic Australia Pty Limited
PO Box 579 Gosford NSW 2250
ABN 11 000 614 577
www.scholastic.com.au

Part of the Scholastic Group
Sydney • Auckland • New York • Toronto • London • Mexico City
New Delhi • Hong Kong • Buenos Aires • Puerto Rico

All rights reserved. No part of this publication may be reproduced or transmitted in any form or by any means, electronic or mechanical, including photocopying, recording, storage in an information retrieval system, or otherwise, without the prior written permission of the publisher, unless specifically permitted under the Australian Copyright Act 1968 as amended.

ISBN 978-1-74383-360-5

Printed in China by RR Donnelley.

Scholastic Australia's policy, in association with RR Donnelley, is to use papers that are renewable and made efficiently from wood grown in responsibly managed forests, so as to minimise its environmental footprint.

10 9 8 7 6 5 4 3 2 1   19 20 21 22 23 / 1

Disney
FROZEN II
Movie Storybook

SCHOLASTIC
SYDNEY AUCKLAND NEW YORK TORONTO LONDON MEXICO CITY
NEW DELHI HONG KONG BUENOS AIRES PUERTO RICO

The Kingdom of Arendelle was once ruled by King Agnarr and Queen Iduna. One night, they told their daughters, Anna and Elsa, tales of elemental spirits that once thrived in the far north of the kingdom in the Enchanted Forest. They also told stories of the Northuldra people and their battle with Arendelle, and of a river that was said to hold all the secrets of the past. The stories drifted the sisters into sleep, to wonderful and exciting dreams.

That night, Anna awoke and ran to the window. She looked outside.

'The sky's awake, so I'm awake, so we have to play!' Anna called to Elsa.

Many years had passed since then. Anna and Elsa had lots of new friends, and Elsa was now the Queen of Arendelle.

One thing the group always made time for was family game night. It was the boys' turn to pair up, and Kristoff was right with every guess.

'Unicorn'

'Oaken!'

But Anna struggled to guess what Elsa was acting out, and she knew something was bothering her sister.

'Are you okay?' Anna asked.

'Just tired,' said Elsa, forcing a smile. 'Good night.' Elsa abruptly left and went to her room.

The truth was, something *was* bothering Elsa. A voice had been calling to her, trying to draw her away from the kingdom.

It seemed as though no-one else could hear it and though she tried, she couldn't silence it.

Anna appeared at Elsa's door. 'You're wearing Mother's scarf,' she said. 'You do that when something's wrong.'

Elsa didn't want to worry Anna, but Anna always had a way of making Elsa feel better, with both her words and her actions. 'What would I do without you?' Elsa asked.

'You'll always have me,' Anna responded. Then she sang their mother's lullaby and Elsa drifted off to sleep.

Later that night, Elsa awoke to the sound of the mysterious voice calling to her once again. She couldn't help feeling curious.

Did the voice belong to someone magical like her?

As Elsa walked down to the fjord, she sang in response to the voice. Then, a thought came to her. Tentatively, she used her magic, tossing snow into the air. Images she had never seen before blossomed from her fingertips and surrounded her—the forest, a reindeer, a little girl.

Fascinated by the imagery she had created, Elsa blasted out her magic and an enormous shockwave swept across the fjord with a boom! The moisture in the sky froze into small crystals that hung suspended in the air.

Elsa was in awe of what she had done.

Anna woke up and raced to the balcony, searching for Elsa.

As the crystals fell, Arendelle transformed. Water stopped flowing; fire vanished; the wind kicked up, pushing villagers out of their homes and the ground rippled like the sea.

The ground rumbled again, but this time it was the mountain trolls rolling through the pass. Grand Pabbie went straight to Elsa.

'Much about the past is not what it seems,' Pabbie said. 'When one can see no future, all one can do is the next right thing.'

To do that, Elsa knew she needed to find the voice. This time, Elsa was not afraid.

At dawn, Anna, Kristoff, Olaf and Sven joined Elsa. They began their journey north.

Up ahead, over a small rise in the road, was a vast wall of glittering mist. Elsa ran straight for it. The others were not far behind her. Elsa stopped a safe distance away, saying nothing as her friends joined her.

Elsa reached for Anna's hand, drawing on her sister's strength. Slowly, the mist parted before them.

'We do this together, okay?' Anna said.

'Together,' Elsa said. 'I promise.'

The mist continued to roll back, revealing four stone monoliths. As they passed the pillars, the mist closed behind Elsa, Anna and their friends, trapping them inside!

The sparkling colours in the mist shifted and aligned, and something about the mist changed. Instead of bouncing the friends off when they touched it, it now pushed them.

Then, the Wind Spirit appeared! It picked up the friends, trapping them in a vortex.

Elsa used her magic to stop a branch from slamming into Anna, which caused the Wind Spirit to push everyone except Elsa out of its grasp. Desperately, Elsa threw a steady stream of snow towards the centre of the vortex.

The wind swirled tighter around Elsa until, finally, she opened her arms, blasting out her powers.

Elsa was released, and the friends found themselves in a forest.

They heard noises coming from the bushes. Anna broke off an ice sword from one of Elsa's sculptures and wielded it in defence as reindeer and people surrounded them.

Before they could react, more people dropped from the trees. Then, soldiers appeared. It was the trapped Northuldra and Arendellians from one of King Agnarr's bedtime stories!

The two sides, still at odds after so many years, ignored Elsa, Anna and their group, and immediately began arguing with each other.

The leader of the Northuldra, Yelana, bickered with the Arendellian lieutenant, Mattias, over who could claim the group as their prisoners. Suddenly, both the Northuldra and the Arendellians rushed towards them. Elsa used her powers, surprising everyone and sending them, sliding and slipping, to the ground.

Anna stared at Mattias, trying to figure out where she knew him from. Finally, she blurted out, 'Library, second portrait on the left. You were our father's official guard.'

Mattias was overjoyed to hear that their father was King Agnarr and that he had made it back to Arendelle before the forest became cursed.

Suddenly, a bright flash appeared.

'Fire Spirit!' Yelana yelled.

A ball of fire dashed around a tree, sending it up in flames. Chaos erupted as it blazed a trail through the forest.

Elsa raced behind it, using her magic to try to stop it from spreading. When she reached it, she saw that the Fire Spirit was actually a small salamander.

Looking deep into the Fire Spirit's eyes, Elsa understood its feelings of pain and fear. She gently held out her hand and it scampered onto her palm. As she helped it find calm, the flames died.

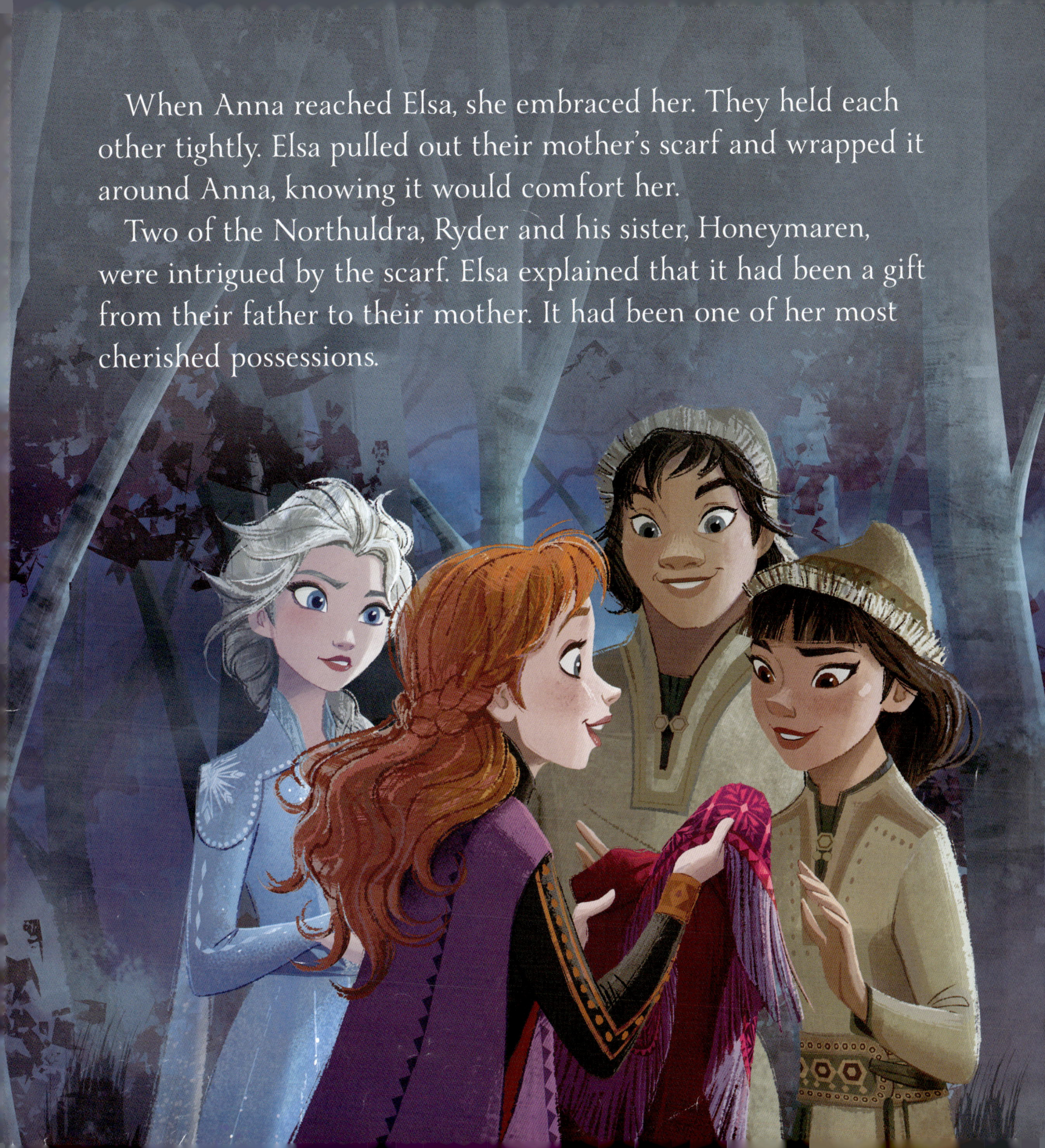

When Anna reached Elsa, she embraced her. They held each other tightly. Elsa pulled out their mother's scarf and wrapped it around Anna, knowing it would comfort her.

Two of the Northuldra, Ryder and his sister, Honeymaren, were intrigued by the scarf. Elsa explained that it had been a gift from their father to their mother. It had been one of her most cherished possessions.

Later, Mattias shared with Anna some wisdom he had learned from his father. 'Just when you think you've found your way, life'll throw you onto a new path.'

Anna knew what came after that—a person just needed to do the next right thing. Mattias nodded, but saw the look of concern on Anna's face as Elsa passed by.

'You look out for her; she's lucky to have you,' Mattias said.

Anna nodded. 'If I lost her, I'd lose myself.'

'That's not how it works,' Mattias said. 'Loss just shows us what we're made of.'

Over by the campfire, Honeymaren showed Elsa the spirits of nature symbolised on the scarf.

Elsa was excited to learn about the symbols and realised that their new friends could teach them a lot. She hoped that the Northuldra and Arendellians would help them on their adventure. Elsa still had a long way to go to find the mysterious voice, and she wouldn't be alone.